It is worth noting that the format, words, and illustrations of this work are only for educational purposes. Any resemblance to actual persons, living or dead, places, or actual events is purely for educational purposes and stylized through creativity and transformative use.

The use of words and illustrations contained therein do not imply sponsorship, endorsement, or commercial association with any person, place, or event depicted. The author, illustrator, editor, and publisher have made reasonable efforts to ensure that the illustrations respect privacy, intellectual property, and publicity rights.

Authored by Kharmon Anderson
Illustrated, Edited, and Published by Dream2Design.org
© 2026
All rights reserved
Printed in the United States of America

All rights reserved. No part of this publication may be reproduced, stored in a retrieval system, or transmitted in any form or by any means, electronic, mechanical, photocopying, or otherwise, without the prior permission of the author.

Acknowledgment

We would like to extend sincere appreciation and gratitude to Reverend Reneé Kessler and the Beck Cultural Exchange Center for their devotion and dedication to preserving Black history in East Tennessee.

Introduction

Welcome to a journey through Knoxville's Black history! This book shares stories that have shaped and intersected our communities. While this book does not contain every story that exists, it's a colorful introduction to some of the lives and legacies in Knoxville and East Tennessee. Some dates and details are best estimates based on what we know today, and that's okay because learning is part of the adventure! Turn the page to explore and celebrate these amazing stories with us!

Aa

A is for Alfredda Delaney.

Ms. Delaney was a city school teacher from Knoxville, Tennessee. She was a community activist and trailblazer for equal opportunity in public and higher education.

Bb

B is for Beauford Delaney.

Mr. Delaney was an artist from Knoxville, Tennessee, who was known for his modernist painting contributions to the Harlem Renaissance.

Cc

C is for Caldonia Fackler "Cal" Johnson.

Mr. Johnson was a formerly enslaved man from Knoxville, Tennessee, who became a businessman and philanthropist. He owned a horse race track and saloon. During the late 19th and early 20th centuries, he was one of the wealthiest African American men in the State of Tennessee. He is recognized as Knoxville's first African American millionaire.

Dd

D is for Dr. J.B. Young and Dr. G.W. Harmen.

In 1869, they were the first African American physicians to open medical offices in Knoxville, Tennessee. Dr. Young was among Knoxville's first African American men to run for mayor in 1872.

Ee

E is for the Eighth of August, 1863.

This was the date that President Andrew Johnson freed enslaved people in the State of Tennessee, while serving as the state's military governor. However, slavery was not officially abolished in the State of Tennessee's Constitution until February 22, 1865. Some people celebrate a holiday, known as Emancipation Day, on August 8. During the Jim Crow era in Knoxville, African Americans were allowed entry into Chilhowee Park one day each year, on August 8th, for Emancipation Day celebrations.

Ff

F is for Fairview Elementary.

This school was established in 1875 in Mechanicsville as the first public school in Knox County for African Americans.

Gg

G is for Gem Theater.

This theater was one of Knoxville's primary African American theaters during segregation. The Gem Theater substantially contributed to the city's African American entertainment and could seat 800 people.

Hh

H is for Harold Middlebrook.

Reverend Middlebrook has faithfully served the Knoxville community through civic and community engagement. He is originally from Memphis, Tennessee, and was a friend of Dr. Martin Luther King, Jr. Mr. Middlebrook was an instrumental leader in the Civil Rights Movement and is known for his significant contributions to civil rights for African Americans and the Christian community.

Ii

I is for Integration of Clinton, Tennessee's public schools.

On August 26, 1956, twelve students, known as *The Clinton 12*, integrated Clinton High School. They were among the first students to integrate a public high school in the South. The Green McAdoo Cultural Center in Clinton, Tennessee, is a museum that commemorates the story of *The Clinton 12*.

J is for Judge William Henry Hastie, Jr.

Judge Hastie was from Knoxville, Tennessee, and he attended Harvard University's School of Law. He became the first African American Federal Judge in 1937, after being appointed by President Franklin Delano Roosevelt to serve the District of the Virgin Islands. Judge Hastie became the first African American Federal Court of Appeals Judge in 1950 in which he served on the Third Circuit. Mr. Hastie was also the first African American governor of the United States Virgin Islands.

K is for Knoxville College.

Knoxville College is the first and sole Historically Black College and University (HBCU) in East Tennessee. It was founded in 1875 by the United Presbyterian Church as a school for freed men and women after the Civil War. This institution is located in Knoxville's Mechanicsville neighborhood.

Ll

L is for Lyons View School.

In approximately 1906, Lyons View School was built to serve the educational needs of African American children. The majority of the students lived in Bearden's African American neighborhoods to include Slatey (near Sutherland Avenue), the Brickyard (near Homberg Drive), and Lyons View (near Lyons View Pike). The school also aided the educational needs of students from Concord's African American community. In 1965, after desegregation, Lyons View School ceased operation. However, the school still remains on Lyons View Pike.

Mm

M is for Maddox.

Forrest "Wing" Maddox was born in 1897 in Fulton County, Georgia. From approximately 1920 to 1922, he was a pitcher and outfielder for the Knoxville Giants, Knoxville's Negro League baseball team. The Knoxville Giants were part of the Negro Southern League. Scholars believe Maddox was the first one-armed baseball player in the Negro Leagues. In 1923, Maddox retired from playing baseball and became a professor at his alma mater, Morehouse College.

Nn

N is for Nikki Giovanni.

Yolande Cornelia "Nikki" Giovanni, Jr., was a poet, author, activist, educator, and native of Knoxville, Tennessee. Although Ms. Giovanni grew up near Cincinnati, Ohio, she spent some of her formative years in Knoxville, Tennessee, to include living with her grandparents and attending Austin High School (now Austin East Magnet High School). Her works have preserved history and culture to include Knoxville's African American community prior to the city's urban renewal projects.

Oo

O is for Oak Ridge 85.

On September 6, 1955, in Oak Ridge, Tennessee, 85 students from the Scarboro community integrated Oak Ridge High School and Robertsville Junior High School.

P is for Paul Hogue.

Paul H. "Duke" Hogue was born and raised in Knoxville, Tennessee. He grew up in East Knoxville's Five Points Community and attend Vine Junior High (now Vine Middle School) and Austin High School. Mr. Hogue was a standout basketball athlete who later attended the University of Cincinnati. While in college, he was a 6'9" center who led the Cincinnati Bearcats to two National College Athletic Association (NCAA) championships in 1961 and 1962. In 1962, Mr. Hogue obtained a bachelor's degree in education and was the number one draft pick for the New York Knicks. In the overall National Basketball Association's (NBA) 1962 draft, he was the first round draft second pick. The City of Knoxville's Paul Hogue Park is named after Mr. Hogue.

Q is for the Quest of William Bennett Scott, Sr.

William Bennett Scott, Sr., created *The Colored Tennessean*, Tennessee's first African American newspaper. Mr. Scott was a free African American man who moved to East Tennessee from North Carolina in 1847. He was a publisher, mayor, and civil rights activist who lived in Friendsville, Knoxville, and Nashville, Tennessee, during the mid to late 19th century. In 1869, he was elected as the first African American mayor of Maryville, Tennessee. Mr. Scott founded the Freedman's Normal Institute in Maryville, Tennessee, which was built in 1872. He was the father of Knoxville's first African American teacher, Laura Ann Scott Cansler, and grandfather of Charles Warner Cansler, a Knoxville based educator, author, and civil rights advocate.

Rr

R is for Robert J. Booker.

Dr. Robert J. Booker grew up in Knoxville, Tennessee and graduated from Austin High School in 1953. He was Knoxville's first African American state representative. In addition, Dr. Booker was a noteworthy graduate of Knoxville College, historian, author, military veteran, and co-founder of the Beck Cultural Exchange Center. Dr. Booker was vital to the research, preservation, and revelation of Knoxville's history, especially Black History.

Ss

S is for Sarah Moore Greene.

Sarah Moore Greene was born in 1910 in Madisonville, Tennessee. Mrs. Greene was the daughter of Ike Moore and Mary Toomey. She was a civil rights activist and educator. Mrs. Greene pioneered early childhood education and served the needs of African American children through the creation of the Sarah Moore Greene Kiddie College in the 1940s at Ebenezer Baptist Church in Knoxville, Tennessee. In 1969, she became the first African American member of the City of Knoxville's school board.

Tt

T is for Theotis Robinson, Jr.

Theotis Robinson, Jr., is from Knoxville, Tennessee, and he is a graduate of Austin High School. He was the first African American undergraduate student to attend the University of Tennessee (UT). Mr. Robinson is a trailblazer and pioneer for equality, diversity, and civil rights. In 1969, Mr. Robinson was elected the first African American city council member in over 50 years. He also served as the UT System's Vice President of Diversity and Equity.

Uu

U is for the Underground railroad cave in Friendsville, Tennessee.

The cave was a hiding place for people who were enslaved and was created by Quakers Wilson J. Hackney and his wife. They helped over 2,000 enslaved people journey to freedom. Some Indigenous American people also offered refuge or helped enslaved people in navigating the trek to freedom.

V is for Vine Avenue.

Vine Avenue and Central Street bordered what formerly contained Knoxville's Black business district, also known as "The Bottom." The Bottom contained Black-owned businesses and community centers. Due to the city's urban renewal projects, the residents and businesses were forced out of this area while homes and buildings were destroyed.

W is for William Francis Yardley.

William Francis Yardley was born in Knoxville, Tennessee, in 1844 as a free African American man. Mr. Yardley was a civil rights pioneer, writer, and politician during the 19th century. In 1872, he passed the bar exam and became Knoxville's first African American lawyer. Mr. Yardley primarily represented African American clients in criminal matters. He was elected as a city alderman, served on Knox County's Court, and was the first African American to run for governor in the State of Tennessee.

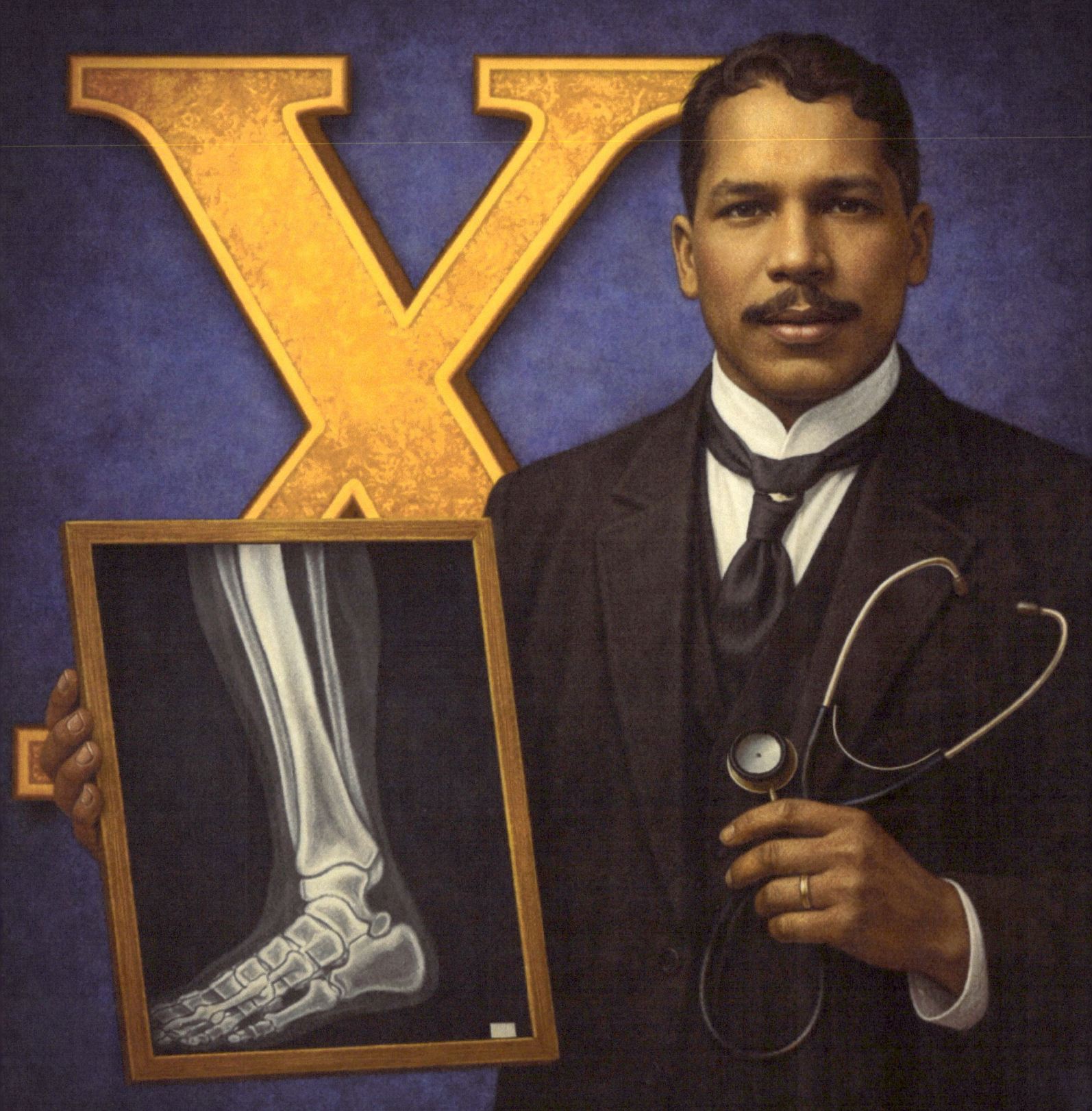

Xx

X is for X-Ray machines installed by Dr. Henry Morgan (H.M.) Green.

Dr. Green installed x-ray machines at his medical practice, the Green Medical Arts Building. Dr. H.M. Green created a private infirmary and an operating room at his medical practice. Prior to 1922 and the establishment of Dr. Green's medical practice, African American residents could only be seen in the basement of Knoxville General Hospital. Dr. H.M. Green was one of the founders of Knoxville Medical College which operated from 1900 to 1910.

Y

SMART **BRAVE**
INSPIRATIONAL BEAUTIFUL
COURAGEOUS **KIND**
CREATIVE IMAGINATIVE
HANDSOME
INTELLECTUAL
STRATEGIC
UNIQUE
POWERFUL
THOUGHTFUL
RESILIENT
COMPASSIONATE
STRONG
POWERFUL

Yy

Y is for You!

YOU can be a leader or a helper in paving and preserving the future of Black history. The future will be influenced by YOU. Who will you be? What will you discover? What will you create to help others? YOU can be a positive influence and make a difference.

Zz

Z is for Zaevion Dobson.

Zaevion Dobson was a student, leader, and football player at Fulton High School in Knoxville, Tennessee. On December 17, 2015, Zaevion died after heroically shielding three girls from a shooting in his neighborhood. He is remembered for his life of boldness, character, and courage. Zaevion's actions earned the 2016 Arthur Ashe Courage Award. Mr. Dobson was the youngest person to receive this award. His mother, Zenobia Dobson, accepted the award on his behalf as she was accompanied by his brothers, Markastin Taylor and Zack Dobson. Zaevion's life is an inspiration for young people and adults. The Zaevion Dobson Memorial Park and Playground are named after Mr. Dobson.

Museums

If you are interested in doing more research or learning more about Black History in the greater Knoxville area and East Tennessee region, please visit the museums and centers listed below.

The Beck Cultural Exchange Center
1927 Dandridge Avenue
Knoxville, Tennessee 37915

Green McAdoo Cultural Center
101 School Street
Clinton, Tennessee 37716

The Tri-County African American Cultural Museum
1069 East Tri County Boulevard
Oliver Springs, Tennessee 37840

Swift Museum
203 West Spring Street
Rogersville, Tennessee 37857

**Bessie Smith Cultural Center and
Chattanooga African American Museum**
200 East Martin Luther King Boulevard
Chattanooga, Tennessee 37403

Sharing These Stories

We're grateful you're holding a copy of A to Z Black History Knoxville.

If you would like to **purchase individual copies,** you can order online at:

AtoZKnoxville.com

If you're interested in **bulk orders of 10 or more copies** for schools, classrooms, churches, organizations, or community groups, discounted rates are available.
Please email us at:

AtoZKnoxville@gmail.com

Thank you for reading, sharing, and helping these stories reach more hands and hearts.

Author Bio

Kharmon Anderson is a writer and speaker whose love for reading and history was ignited by her grandmother. During childhood, Ms. Anderson's grandmother sent her books of all kinds, especially history. These books opened doors of possibilities to new worlds, ideas, and opportunities.

Ms. Anderson's grandmother was a lifelong educator in the rural South who also partook in boycotts during the Civil Rights Movement. Her grandmother taught the value of respect, and showed her how love and service can unite people and transform lives.

Today, Ms. Anderson shares stories of inspiration and encouragement, inviting readers to explore, dream, and carry forward a legacy of hope, love, and unity. To continue exploring history visit, **CoachKhistory.com.**